WORKPLACE ANXIETY

HOW TO REFUEL AND RE-ENGAGE

SONIA LAYNE-GARTSIDE

WORKPLACE ANXIETY: HOW TO REFUEL AND RE-ENGAGE

The information provided within this book is for general informational and educational purposes only. The author makes no representations or warranties, express or implied, about the completeness, accuracy, reliability, suitability or availability with respect to the information, products, services, or related graphics contained in this book for any purpose. Any use of this information is at your own risk.

WORKPLACE ANXIETY: HOW TO REFUEL AND RE-ENGAGE
© 2020 Sonia Layne-Gartside

All rights reserved. No part of this publication may be recorded, stored in a retrieval system, or transmitted in any form or by any means, electronic, mechanical, photocopying, recording, or otherwise, without prior written permission from the publisher.

ISBN-13: 978-0-578-65690-8

Published by Sonia Layne-Gartside
Pittsburgh, PA 15206

Printed in the United States of America
First Edition April 2020

Cover and Interior Design by Make Your Mark Publishing Solutions
Editing by Make Your Mark Publishing Solutions

CONTENTS

Overcoming Doubt: It's Time to Stop Pretending!   ix
Foreword: What You Need to Know about a Changing Workplace   xi

SECTION 1: Harness Your Anxiety

Chapter 1:	The Mindset That Will (Quickly) Improve Your Work	1
Chapter 2:	Three Awesome Tips to Make You Comfortable with Uncertainty	7
Chapter 3:	These Powerful Quotes Will Transform Your Work Life	16

SECTION 2: Unleash Your Powers

Chapter 4:	How to Complete Your Personal Development Plan	27
Chapter 5:	This Is Why You Need to Empower Yourself	29
Chapter 6:	Expert Advice—Do You Know What Great Negotiators Do?	32
Chapter 7:	Feeling Stuck in Life? How to Get Moving ... Fast	37
Chapter 8:	How to Really Listen Better to Engage People	40

Chapter 9: How to Channel Anger in a Healthy and Powerful Way ... 47
Chapter 10: Bottom Line—How to Thrive in a Bureaucracy ... 49

SECTION 3: Roar

Chapter 11: Mindful? Or Is Your Mind Unusually Full ... 57
Chapter 12: Actually, This Is Why You're Not at Peak Productivity ... 61
Chapter 13: How to Deal with the Messy Middle—Practical Advice ... 66

SECTION 4: Leading a Company to Success

Chapter 14: How to Lead In an Uncertain World ... 75
Chapter 15: How to Harness Organizational Chaos during Transitions ... 82
Chapter 16: How to Give Feedback That Gets Results without Conflict ... 89
Chapter 17: This Will Make You a Clear Communicator ... 96
Chapter 18: This Is Why Great Leaders Focus on Customer Service ... 98
Chapter 19: How to Become a More Awesome Leader ... 101

SECTION 5: Conclusion

Chapter 20: The Year Ahead—What Do You Need to Prosper? ... 107

Endnotes ... 111

DEDICATION

To every stressed out woman struggling in the workplace. Remember that work doesn't have to make us miserable. You will overcome.

OVERCOMING DOUBT
IT'S TIME TO STOP PRETENDING!

The modern workplace often evokes feelings of anxiety in every one of us. You could feel queasy from the stress of trying to finish all your work, or you may feel like a hamster on a wheel, toiling every day in obscurity. You could feel like you're being overworked and underappreciated as you struggle to figure out how to demonstrate your value to others, or you could feel frustrated that you have little to no influence to make anything happen in your company. Many leaders often wonder, *Am I good enough? Am I doing enough of the right things?* Of course, that anxiety lies in the fear of failure, the fear that your job is changing and the unknown of what that could mean for you and your success.

When was the last time you did something truly difficult? When was the last time you didn't get what you wanted? Have you ever been in a situation where you felt unsure or unworthy, like you didn't know enough or weren't good enough?

Doubt is normal and necessary. The idea that everything should come quickly is bogus. You need to get more comfortable with your story. *Own* your fear of failing and try one or all of the following to help ease those feelings: Figure out another way to make it work. Figure out how to work better with people. Figure out how to collaborate more. Figure out how to build a more supportive team.

The very best way to grow is to be aware of what you don't know and do the necessary training to get better. Stop pretending. It's not necessary.

FOREWORD
WHAT YOU NEED TO KNOW ABOUT A CHANGING WORKPLACE

In our changing workplaces, we are often called to be more adaptive. Millions of us will eventually need to switch occupations or build new skills as our careers and the industries we work in evolve. While this will open up countless opportunities, it will also be a breeding ground for uncertainty and unpredictability. Thriving in this kind of environment will require you to deliberately focus on the social and emotional skills that help you learn and unlearn as necessary, tap into your creativity, and improve your ability to connect, partner, and collaborate. This book is a call to action, a collection of guideposts that lay out how to master these critical social and emotional skills.

As an executive coach, master trainer, and a learning specialist, my goal is to help people improve their performance in areas key to their competitiveness and success. Every week, I help people gain more confidence in short and easy ways. One of the things I help people realize is that when you rely on the trainings and performance management systems in your organization, you unknowingly outsource your development. You hand off your success and competitiveness to managers and HR personnel. Well-intentioned as they are, these people don't really know anything about your specific motivations and needs for engagement. Your development is, in essence, owned by someone else, whether it's HR, your training department, or your managers. You end up becoming a passenger in your own developmental journey, being sent to potentially unnecessary trainings instead of taking it upon yourself to collaborate with others, see the need for a specific training, and actively seek it out for yourself.

This book is about taking back your ability to compete and own your development. HR, external experts, and managers are resources you can take advantage of, but *you* own this journey.

Your work environment can make or break you. In taking back control, you will reap the benefits of shaping your environment and playing to your strengths. The results will be three-fold: (1) You will increase your commitment to your career and family, (2) you will become less resistant to change and more focused on embracing the opportunities for positive changes, and (3) you will begin to take the initiative to improve the systems and processes that generate positive energy in your life.

Let's go!

SECTION 1
HARNESS YOUR ANXIETY

"The stupid are cocksure, while the intelligent are full of doubt."

—Bertrand Russell

CHAPTER 1
THE MINDSET THAT WILL (QUICKLY) IMPROVE YOUR WORK

> *"The relationship we have with our people and the culture of our company is our most sustainable competitive advantage."*
> —Howard Schultz, former executive chairman of Starbucks

This quote epitomizes what most leaders credit as the "key to success" in business. It's a variation of the phrase "People are our most important asset." Today, it is widely championed that employees' decisions, experiences, and abilities make the difference between success and failure. Appearing to confirm this, a recent Gallup study[1] found that companies with engaged employees bring in 21% higher profitability, and a 2017 analysis[2] published in *Harvard Business Review* found that companies who invest in the employee experience are four times more profitable than those that don't. People are now considered the great differentiator in successful organizations.

This is why the most profitable companies—Google,

Facebook, and Apple—seek to hire the best people and then spend time and money giving them what they want—not just need—to be productive. A casual glance into these companies will show that they court engineers similar to how athletic agents go after future first-round draft picks. The difference a great engineer can make in a company like Google or Facebook is equivalent to having Lionel Messi on your soccer team, Serena Williams on your tennis team, or Stephen Curry on your basketball team. These conglomerates recognize that, like star athletes, employees (in this case, engineers) make the biggest impact on their success, and they pay close attention to their level of engagement. Unfortunately, most company practices do not reflect this level of people-driven focus. When looking at the majority of companies, the evidence points to a completely different narrative. Spoiler alert: We're not all treated like first-round draft picks.

MILLIONS SPENT ON EMPLOYEE ENGAGEMENT WITHOUT ANY RETURN

According to the analytics polling firm Gallup, employee engagement has barely budged from 34% in well over a decade. However, in 2019, Gallup[3] found that the percentage of U.S. employees engaged at work had risen to 35%. The majority (65%) were either not engaged or actively disengaged. The reason for this, a Dale Carnegie[4] global study found, was because leaders have many blind spots when it comes to engaging their employees. These blind spots seem to center around the need for leaders to be open, honest, and trustworthy. For example, in this study, 81% of employees said it is important for leaders to admit when they're wrong, but only 40% of supervisors actually do it consistently. When a leader is honest and trustworthy with others, employees are ten times more likely to be satisfied in their job.

> *"The conditions under which men and women labor are as important as the amount they get paid."*
> —Robert J. Gordon

That need for honesty and openness resonates strongly with lots of employees. I once was training a client who was so frustrated with leadership communication and trustworthiness that he did not bother to complete his company's employee satisfaction survey. When the results were presented at a company meeting, it was purportedly based on 100% participation in their department. It was a small department, and given my client had not completed the survey, there was no way there could have been 100% participation. From his perspective, the results presented meant that not only did his input not matter, it wasn't even missed. Too many employees are walking around feeling invisible and/or hopeless.

This 2019 study[5] conducted by polling firm Tinypulse is one of many that suggests it is not compensation nor benefits that is the problem for many companies, it is the culture, interpersonal relationships, and work environment that employees find to be lacking. Employees do not feel valued at work; they feel disconnected from their peers in other departments (company silos can be blamed for this), and many rate their organizations' performance review systems poorly.

So what does this mean for those of us smart enough to recognize that we can't all be treated like first-round draft picks? How can we stay engaged at work while giving companies what they want and positioning ourselves to be great differentiators? Smart employees approach these questions by changing their mindset and recognizing that while most companies know people are important, they don't often invest in making the necessary changes to back it up with actions, unless the employee is viewed as a superstar performer.

NEW MINDSET: IT'S NOT YOU THAT'S IMPORTANT, IT'S YOUR OUTPUT

As much as businesses try to instill the feeling among employees that they are the "most important asset" for the organization, the truth is *we* are not important. What's important is our productivity and ability to help the organization meet its goals. Once we can no longer help an organization meet its goals effectively and efficiently, we will be asked to leave. It's the nature of business, and oftentimes, it is not personal. Smart employees work accordingly. They know if they can demonstrate consistently high productivity and continued success in achieving the company's goals, they are in a position to ask for what they want (and need) from any organization. If their efforts, talents, and judgements are not being valued, then they will fire the organization and move on to one that values their output.

THE KEY TO THRIVING: LEARNING AND UNLEARNING

With this mindset, the ability to learn and unlearn is one of the main keys to excelling and thriving. The growth and development that comes from learning new skills will keep you ahead of the pack. It's critical to understand that training means nothing unless you can apply the learned skills and knowledge to problems and opportunities at work.

Sometimes this will mean unlearning those things that are no longer working for you. This can be difficult. When we have established ways of doing things that have led us to success in the past, the weight of that previous knowledge and success can hold us back and trip us up. It doesn't mean you have to toss out all the knowledge you have gained from your collected experiences; it just requires that you stay open to different ways of getting things done.

Personally, I know I often resist moving forward when I find a change to be difficult. This knowledge about myself is a signal that I need to unlearn and upgrade whatever belief, mindset, or skill set is holding me back.

> *"There is no future in any job. The future lies in the person who holds the job."*
> —George Crane

Finally, the reality of today's workplace is that your

engagement is in your hands. It's all on you. Have confidence in yourself. By altering your mindset and continuously upgrading your skills and knowledge, you can drive your career forward much better than any HR department can. Is that scary, liberating, or empowering to you?

CHAPTER 2
THREE AWESOME TIPS TO MAKE YOU COMFORTABLE WITH UNCERTAINTY

Ten years ago, I got married. I left everyone I knew behind to move to another country where I only knew one person, my new husband. I left behind a successful career built upon decades of hard work to come to a country where I had to completely start over. So, just like everyone else, I've experienced uncertainty.

Any change we experience in life—a switch in our routine, a new opportunity, or a new way of doing things—triggers fear in our brain. If you want to get technical, the amygdala[6] is the part of the brain that dictates our fear of the unknown. Every time you move away from your safe and familiar routines or encounter any type of uncertainty, your amygdala will trigger fear and anxiety. How we deal with it is a very personal thing.

For example, I'm afraid of heights, but I have still bungee jumped off bridges and skyscrapers. I'm also an extremely weak swimmer (I failed swim class), yet I've been out of my comfort zone on a jet ski, and I have been kayaking, even though the instructor judged me in a very disdainful manner for briefly panicking about potentially drowning. I wasn't really in any danger of drowning, but when you're uncertain in life, you magnify even the slightest risks.

In every case, whether bungee jumping or quitting my job, I learned something that I apply to all aspects of my life. You can call it my "what I know for sure" moment. Life is uncertain, and that uncertainty brings a tremendous amount of fear, which will chase you into open and unknown spaces. But with the right approach and an ability to stay focused on the opportunities before you, the experiences you originally greeted with fear can lead to some of the best breaks in life. There is beauty to be found in open and unknown spaces.

In this chapter, I am going to share a few tips on how you should approach living in volatility, uncertainty, complexity, and ambiguity, particularly as we are prone to negativity bias.[7] How can we become more adaptable and resilient when facing circumstances that have the potential to knock us off our defined path to success?

> *"May your choices reflect your hopes, not your fears."*
>
> **—Nelson Mandela**

We already know that our brains are hardwired to be fearful and anxious when presented with uncertainty, and for every individual, some level of fear and worry is necessary. Unlike organizations, where change can happen slowly, for individuals, change can hit like a bullet train. We all know someone who was faithful to a job for over ten years, only to be told they were no longer needed. That person will tell you there was no warning. This is what uncertainty can mean to an individual, and why the fear that accompanies changes in organizations is legitimate. During periods of change, employees are correct to ask if there is a place for them in any new transition because sometimes there isn't. That is life.

However, in my experience, I have found that you cannot let fear dictate your choices. Yes, some fear and worry can be healthy, and anticipating danger and taking preventative action is what makes us adaptive. But too much focus on our fears can increase anxiety, impair our judgement, and hinder good decision-making.

TIP #1: DON'T ACT ON YOUR FEARS.

Let's say your leaders have recently announced a new operating system for the organization. The objective is to improve operations to ensure new growth. However, your leaders suck at explaining the vision behind the move, and beyond a basic explanation of the new system, no one knows what or when anything will happen next. Instead of telling yourself, *This new system they want to introduce will never work. They don't know what they are doing and will only cause me to do more work for less money,* which may be true, you need to acknowledge the underlying fear this uncertainty is causing within you. *My fear is that if you improperly implement this new system, I will not be able to navigate it as successfully as I do the current one, and I will not only lose my current gains, I might also get fired.* Once you have recognized your fears, you must be willing to change your perspective.

- Determine if your fears are rational or irrational. Remember my kayaking story and how I thought I was going to drown? That was an irrational fear. I was looking out toward a sea full of turbulent waves, feeling uncertain, and I thought, at any moment, the kayak would overturn and I would be a castaway, lost at sea. The instructor had to tell me to turn my head, look back to the shore, and see that we were not that far away. I was letting my fears overwhelm me. Where are you looking in your period of uncertainty? Like me, do you need to turn your head (i.e. change your perspective) to see a completely different and more realistic view of the situation? Your perspective not only changes what you see but also what you do and what you create in your life.

- If it is a rational fear, then determine what your hopes are for the situation. Write down the answer to this question: What do I hope to learn and gain from this situation? When you have your list of hopes, focus your energies on figuring out how you can accomplish them. In our example, your hope may be to simply not get fired, so problem-solve how you can avoid that. Perhaps you could find out more about the proposed change, determine what new skills and abilities you will need, seek training that will fill your skill gaps, talk to people in your network who have gone through similar changes, or volunteer to be on a committee for the new system. The more you familiarize yourself with the thing you do not know, the more your fears will disappear.

Feeling fear doesn't mean things are not working out; oftentimes, the bigger your goals, the bigger your fears. But you do not get over fear by sitting back and waiting for it to subside. You reduce anxiety by acting on the hopes and goals you have for the situation. Be guided by what you want to accomplish, not what you wish to avoid.

> *"Our anxiety does not come from thinking about the future, but wanting to control it."*
> —**Kahlil Gibran**

Often, the worries we have during periods of uncertainty begin with us trying to control people and events we simply don't have much control over. I learned that lesson when I first went bungee jumping. For those of us who are afraid of heights, you would think the scariest part is looking down just before you jump. That's extremely scary, but what's even scarier is when you first jump off. You instinctively try to control and direct how you fall, but jumping off a building more than 1000 feet in the air and trying to control gravity as you fall does not work. In that situation, I had no control. I could control when and how I jumped off, but my free fall was up to gravity. In life, it's the same way.

TIP #2: FOCUS YOUR TIME, ENERGY, AND EFFORTS ON WHAT YOU CAN CONTROL.

People who focus their time, energy, and efforts on the things they can control experience fewer negative reactions to uncertainty and tend to be more proactive. As humans, we like to have everything under our control, but true resilience and grit is found in overcoming challenges. When I was trying to convince someone to hire me here in America, there were certain things I had no control over, like my lack of a professional network. (A survey reveals 85% of all jobs are filled via networking.[8]) But I chose to focus on the things I could control instead, like setting up informational interviews, figuring out how I could leverage my existing skills and experience to find the job I wanted, and searching for opportunities to network. Focusing on what I could control meant I had to:

- **Cultivate the right mindset.** Instead of focusing on my perceived barriers, I needed to focus on the opportunities at hand and remain positive. That meant adjusting my attitude and remembering to be grateful. After all, I made a choice to move, and that, in itself, is a privilege. Unlike many other immigrants, I was not escaping a war-torn country on a life raft. Being grateful meant I could remain positive and take continuous, empowered actions to make things happen.
- **Be flexible.** There is beauty in the pivot. Because I couldn't control everything, there were times when things didn't

go as planned, and I had to accept that. I needed to be open to shifting course when it became useful to do so or when new information made it necessary. I couldn't lose focus and become flustered every time things didn't go my way. Yes, it was disappointing, but I chose to conserve my energy, so I could figure out how I was going to pivot. For example, it did not take me long to realize that most company's application sites were black holes that sucked applications into oblivion, never to be referred to again except for the initial acknowledgement of receipt. I had to pivot—and fast. If I was interested in a job, I first had to find the recruiter, talk to them to determine if that was a job I should be applying for, and in the process, secure a real person I could follow up with. During periods of uncertainty, you need to bend without breaking, endure setbacks without being derailed, and become more flexible and alert in the process. This means you need to know what your goals are without being attached to how you achieve them. When any shifts occur, your first instinct should be to look at it with an eye toward how you can make it work for you.

> *"I don't like to gamble, but if there's one thing I'm willing to bet on, it's myself."*
>
> —**Beyoncé**

Bet on yourself. Why should anyone invest in you if you have not invested in yourself first? During changes, transitions, or disruptions in life, too many people are made to feel that what they have and who they are is not enough. You have no control over how others view you, but it's not about what your spouse, friends, or family think. During periods of uncertainty, you need to be your own champion and cheerleader.

TIP #3: GET RID OF YOUR NONBELIEF.

Our lives are in a constant state of flux, but we are often so hungry for certainty that we don't take risks, and we choose to cling to jobs, people, and routines that make us unhappy and unhealthy because we are skeptical. I need you to get rid of your skepticism. You know where you are and where you need to go, but you lack the belief that you can handle the obstacles. Self-belief is essential in seeing opportunities, being decisive, and taking fast action amidst change. Sometimes it is the only thing carrying us forward and sustaining us when nothing goes as planned. To do this, consistently work on the following:

- **Stop beating yourself up.** Replace negative self-talk with positive thoughts. First, recognize when you are telling yourself something is too hard or things will never work out for you, and replace it with positive thoughts about yourself and what you are doing. Stop comparing yourself to everyone else. Stop filtering out all the good you've accomplished in life. Make a list to remind yourself of your history of success—all the things you have succeeded at in the past and all the things you have done that were hard. We all have done hard things; keep reminding yourself of that.

- **Develop resiliency.** Everyone has failed at some point. Successful people learn how to process failure, and many see it as a stepping stone. If you want to get better at something, you have to keep doing it, make mistakes, make adjustments, and improve over time. Focus on the lessons you have learned from your setbacks. Adopt a growth mindset[9] and invest in your learning and development. Instead of saying, *I really sucked at that networking event*, tell yourself, *I'm going to learn how to network better.*

- **Clear your space.** Stop hanging around people who drain your energy and only see the negative in life. Our success is directly linked to the people we are closest to, and many of the people you start your journey with should not be at the finish line. You cannot hang around people who have no goals, no drive, and an inability to spot opportunities and get the best out of life. Clear out the people and routines that clog up your life.

One of the hardest things to deal with is uncertainty. It takes us out of our comfort zone and takes away our control. But if you follow these three tips, you will become much more comfortable planning for and managing it.

CHAPTER 3
THESE POWERFUL QUOTES WILL TRANSFORM YOUR WORK LIFE

Are you feeling burned out and unmotivated? Unsure of your career path? Alternatively, are you excited and passionate about your job? Are you thrilled with the stage you are at in your career? Are you looking to keep getting better? No matter where you are and how you feel about your work life right now, the following six quotes can energize you for the next big push to do more meaningful work.

> *"There is nothing as powerful as a changed mind. You can change your hair, your clothing, your address, your spouse, your residence. But if you don't change your mind, the same experience will perpetuate itself over and over again because everything outwardly changed, but nothing inwardly changed."*
>
> —T.D. Jakes

If you are feeling unsure about where to go next or you're simply trying to turn your work life around, it will require a mindset shift to do so. We all want to be inspired at work, but we do not always prepare our minds for the disruption and change that comes with meaningful work. If your career is on fire and you are getting rave reviews and are in line for a promotion, heading to that next level will also require a mindset shift. We often ask for blessings in our careers, but we do not always prepare our minds to manage the blessing.

This quote reminds me that the assumptions and beliefs that unconsciously guide my behavior are critical for going further in my success journey, rebounding from failure, or deftly pivoting amidst change. Everything begins in our minds, and sometimes we first have to learn to go beyond our mind's barriers before we can make something happen. When you are seeking to impact your work life, start first by identifying which mindset changes you need to develop to improve or continue being successful.

> *"It is possible to commit no mistakes and still lose. That is not a weakness. That is life."*
> —Captain Jean-Luc Picard

This may seem depressing, but I actually find it quite empowering. To me, this quote reinforces that success doesn't come from avoiding failure but rather knowing how to navigate through it. Can you navigate through failure? Do you know how to operate when you are unable to see where you are going and if what you are doing will make a difference? If you can navigate through that, you are on your way to having the greatest successes of your life.

Failure does not have to be fatal. It is not a weakness; it is simply a part of life. Successful people are intimately familiar with it and use it as a stepping stone. The most important thing is planning how you are going to deal with the feelings that come with failure (a mindset change is often needed here). In Hollywood, for example, failure is seen as a badge of honor. But, most of us probably identify more with what Kendall Jenner said after the Pepsi commercial debacle: *"I just feel so stupid."* Some people may prefer the Hollywood, fail fast, "badge of honor" mindset, but I prefer to focus on how I can learn, adjust, and get better from the experience.

> *"In business, as in life, you don't get what you deserve; you get what you negotiate."*
> —Dr. Chester Karrass

The person sitting next to you who does the same job (and probably not as well) or the person reporting to you (the one you trained) could be earning more money than you. It happens more than we think in organizations. We all love taking advantage of a sale and getting a quality product or service at a cheaper price; organizations do as well. (There is a reason employees are discouraged from discussing their salaries.) Do your research, so you know your worth, and always negotiate your salary, whether it is the norm in your organization or not. What do you want? Flex time, more autonomy, more growth opportunities, more say in decision-making? Then negotiate for it. For every negotiation, ask yourself four questions to be at your best: What are my goals for this negotiation? Why are they important to me? Who am

WORKPLACE ANXIETY

I dealing with? What will it take to persuade them given the answers to the first two questions?

> *"A great idea or solution is only as strong as the follow-through."*
> —Chris Cunningham

Let me state the obvious: Simply expecting or demanding something gets done will not get it done. How many times have new ideas or projects been started in your organization with countless meetings held on the issue? It often starts with great fanfare, only to peter out because of poor follow-up and follow-through. How many times have you said you needed to change jobs or careers, then did not follow through? The art of following up and following through is a critical skill for success. This quote reminds me that it's important to follow through on my promises, and it's unreasonable to ask for more (opportunities, access, etc.) if I have not followed through and mastered the work I currently have.

> *"It's not what you don't know that's killing you, it's what you pretend to know."*
> —Steven Furtick

> *"Growth doesn't stop when you've become successful; that's when it starts."*
> —Jay-Z

A pastor and a rapper are essentially saying the same thing: Growth, personal development, and self-improvement are for life. Have you ever been in situations where you felt unsure and unworthy, like you didn't know enough or were not good enough? The best way to get rid of these feelings is to be aware of what you do not know and commit to doing the training and growth work needed to get better. Never pretend. It is not necessary. Get better by attending a class or a webinar, reading a book or an article, or asking questions. As a trainer and coach, I help people get better in short, easy ways, so I know successful people do not pretend; they invest in themselves. Never let your skills flatline. It is absolutely OK to invest time, money, energy, and effort into making yourself better.

> *"You know all those things you've always wanted to do? You should go do them."*
>
> —**Lara Casey**

This quote reminds me to stop complaining, stop talking about what I want to do, and actually get out there and do it. Are you waiting to start a business, get that degree, or retire by a certain age? High achievers know the power of starting. Everything you want is on the other side of that first step. Trust yourself, then start small and go big. In other words, take the steps you can to get what you want, even if they are small. Eventually, those small steps will add up to the achievement of big goals.

These seven quotes really energize me and keep me focused on my journey; I hope they do the same for you. In honor of taking steps toward our best, most confident selves, I will end with a bonus quote for you.

WORKPLACE ANXIETY

"When we are happy, then we are more likely to see beyond our narrow, inward-looking, and self-centered perspective and focus on others' needs and wants."

—Tal Ben-Shahar

Strive to be happy. Chronically unhappy people feed off of negativity and dysfunction at work and try to spread it around. Do your best to ensure you are not one of them by continuing to set goals, learn, and improve. I try to engage in activities that are both pleasurable and meaningful; it helps me feel more content on my journey.

Educator Tal Ben-Shahar is a strong proponent of engaging in happiness boosters, which are activities, lasting anywhere from a few minutes to a few hours, that provide you with meaning, pleasure, and both future and present benefits. A few of my happiness boosters are reading to satisfy my curiosity, engaging in great conversations over good food, laughing, watching an episode of my favorite comedy show, and getting in 15,000 steps a day. Now, list a few of your happiness boosters and try to incorporate them into your everyday life.

Questions to Ponder

"Within you now is the power to do things you never dreamed possible. This power becomes available to you just as soon as you change your beliefs."
—Dr. Maxwell Maltz

Identify which mindset changes are necessary to achieve the success you are seeking. What beliefs are holding you back? What are your happiness boosters?

_____
_____
_____
_____
_____
_____
_____
_____
_____
_____
_____
_____
_____
_____
_____

SECTION 2
UNLEASH YOUR POWERS

"Everything that is sleeping in you, wake it up."
—Nayyirah Waheed

THE AWESOME POWER OF TIME

The concept of time often invokes fear, a fear of losing time, wasting it, or not having enough. Your anxiety is normal but unproductive. Time is not a renewable resource or something that should be squandered by pursuing activities that don't fuel your passions and values. Use your time well and redirect your fear and anxiety. With these four affirmations, you are being called to awaken the talents within you and harness the power of time.

- I can get better over time.
- I'm not afraid to pivot. I can try new strategies and seek input from others when I am stuck.
- I can learn and grow from challenges, setbacks, and feedback.
- Awesome is possible.

Truly internalizing these beliefs will allow you to harness a subtle and quiet power. Instead of time being your enemy, it now represents how far you've come, how much you have learned, and how much better you are today than you were yesterday.

CHAPTER 4
HOW TO COMPLETE YOUR PERSONAL DEVELOPMENT PLAN

When it comes to personal development, most people are on their own. Not everyone has a boss or mentor who is invested in their growth. If you do, count your blessings, but for the rest of us, if you want to feel more confident and approach your work with more assurance and less anxiety, you need to determine what your developmental needs are and create a plan on how to get better. How do you do that? How do you think about your life more proactively? Here are the first steps I often take with clients.

1. We identify the **competencies** that are most important for getting the results they want. What do you need to accomplish in your current or future position? I often spend time in this step to accurately clarify the role they need to play and the added value they need to bring, either to their current or future position, to realize success.

2. Next, we identify the **skills, mindset, and knowledge** needed to perform those competencies effectively and excel. Most people recognize and prioritize the need for additional skills and knowledge, but not many realize they may need to change their mindset as well. What you tell yourself and the way you perceive situations and people affect your success and your ability to do your job well. There is nothing more powerful than a changed mind.

3. Then, we work on how to **acquire, develop, and/or improve** those necessary skills, mindsets, and knowledge. This section is highly customized, as the approach varies based on the individual's lifestyle and learning preferences.

4. Finally, we discuss how to feel more empowered, negotiate better, improve motivation, listen better, deal with anger, and survive a potentially toxic work environment.

Your personal development is critically important to how you handle change, live without limits, and go for your dreams, so make it one of your priorities. What steps are you willing to take to design the life you want?

CHAPTER 5
THIS IS WHY YOU NEED TO EMPOWER YOURSELF

> *"When I hear people say, 'Well, that's just not the way we do things,' my hair stands up. You have to be careful not to let success breed a one-dimensional way of thinking."*
> —Mark Parker, CEO of Nike

There's a learning curve to success. If you're not careful, your current level of success can stop you from growing and moving forward. Companies that are successful and grow rapidly often face this dilemma. "This is the way we do things around here" has led to much success, but it has also been the mantra of many now-extinct companies, like Borders, Blockbuster, and Arthur Andersen, to name a few.

From a personal perspective, we all know growth doesn't stop when you've become successful; that's when it really starts. To continue to thrive, you have to stay flexible, adaptable, and responsive. You have to be able to identify and address critical problems and implement solutions in a timely manner. In a time when most of us are working in organizations where there can be a sense of futility about trying new ways of doing things, how can you accomplish this? Here are a few tips:

1. **Have a bias toward results.** Too often, we are told to act, to just do it, to get out there and start now. This behavior builds a bias toward action rather than results. The consequence is frenetic energy, being busy but not productive. People in this situation often find that they did a lot of work but nothing good happened; they didn't accomplish what they intended to. Stop blindly following processes and consider what needs to be done to get the results you want.

2. **Focus on core priorities.** Identify the activities that will produce your desired results. We are often given too much to do with limited resources to make it work. You can no longer depend on any one person to examine your work and establish these priorities for you. You will have to exercise independent judgement by setting the core priorities that relate to the vision of your company and goals. Vision is everything. Know the vision of your company and how it relates to your goals, then let that drive you as you establish your core priorities.

3. **Empower yourself.** Whenever you are handed responsibility for something, be sure to ask for the authority to act. This is the highest level of authority you can achieve. Don't settle for the authority to inform and initiate (level two) or the authority to recommend

(level one). Negotiate for the highest level of authority every time.

Responsibility + Authority = Empowerment to Get Results

Acting on these tips together will increase your chances of resolving critical problems in a timely manner. Be sure to also empower the people who work with and for you.

CHAPTER 6
EXPERT ADVICE—DO YOU KNOW WHAT GREAT NEGOTIATORS DO?

In my leadership development work, I always start negotiation skills sessions with a little exercise. I ask leaders to:

1. Think back over the past week and identify the number of times they were engaged in a negotiation.
2. When they look at the negotiations in which they've been involved, ask *Am I happy with the outcomes of my recent negotiations?*
3. Then, ask *Do I feel I've missed opportunities to negotiate?*

In my experience, the last question is often the most important one. We often miss opportunities to negotiate, and these missed negotiations are just as costly as if you had negotiated badly.

When it comes to negotiations, I'm guided by Dr. Chester Karrass's book *In Business as in Life—You Don't Get What You Deserve, You Get What You Negotiate.*[10] In his book, Karrass says negotiation plays a critical role in everything we do. It determines your salary, the power balance in your relationships, and the influence and leverage you have in your organization. We negotiate all the time. We may not realize it, but on a personal and professional level, opportunities to negotiate present themselves every day. Whether you're talking to your husband or wife about which movie you'll watch tonight or you're chatting with the cable company about your bill, we are constantly negotiating with one another. You either do it well or you do it badly, but you do it nonetheless. Negotiations are unavoidable. If you don't recognize this nor when you are actually in a negotiation, it will cost you.

In practical terms, what do good negotiators know and practice that we don't? The most important ingredient appears to be planning and preparing well for all negotiations. Sometimes you have more time to prepare than others. You may have two weeks to prepare for a salary negotiation or two minutes to decide the best way to negotiate your way out of an argument. Either way, you still must plan the negotiation, and sometimes you have to do it very quickly. Here are my top three tips:

1. DETERMINE YOUR GOALS.

Goals are critical in negotiations. Everything you say and do should be guided by what will bring you closer to achieving your goals. Always begin your preparation by determining what your goals are and why they are important to you. Do the research (prices, processes, resources, etc.) and know why you want something. Gather external standards; the more factual information you can present, the more airtight your case will be. Research[11] shows people who enter negotiations with high expectations and clear goals emerge with better results, so write down specific objectives. If you don't have much time, take a minute to think about it. If necessary, tell the person you're negotiating with to give you a moment to collect your thoughts.

After you've set your goals, take the time to prioritize them. Prioritizing your goals gives you more freedom to respond quickly and accurately if the situation changes in your negotiation. This is very likely to happen, as most negotiations have multiple issues and concerns, and the exchange itself can move very quickly. For example, you may be preparing to negotiate with your boss for a better title and salary. You've done the research that demonstrates (in your view) that the work you've been producing calls for a director label and a higher salary. Which one is more important to you, the title or the salary?

You should know this ahead of time, so you can accurately and rapidly respond if your boss indicates that raising your salary can be done, but a new title can't be guaranteed. Which one is better for your career? In your research, did you find that you need the title change to get in a better position for more advanced jobs? Is the salary upgrade the only reason you're going after the title change? You don't want to make the wrong concession in the heat of the moment.

Great negotiators begin negotiations with a sharp understanding of what their goals are and why their goals are important to them. They do this so they can make smart trade-offs during the conversation. So, before entering a negotiation or making your case, clarify the reasons behind your goals and do the research to back up those reasons.

2. KNOW WHO YOU ARE DEALING WITH.

Negotiations are never only about you; they're also about the other party. So in preparation for your negotiation, you should ask the same questions about the other party that you ask of yourself: What are their goals and priorities? This requires research and metaphorically putting yourself in their shoes to imagine what they want, especially if you are looking for a win-win, collaborative experience. Plan what you would do in their position, examine what alternatives they have, determine whether they have the power to make the deal you want, and think about who else is affected by the negotiation and what their approach is most likely to be. Create situations where you get to know your counterparts. You want to establish as much trust as possible. No matter how many facts or how much expertise you have, valuing the perceptions and emotions of the other party is more important in persuading them than anything you say or propose.

If you're in an unexpected negotiation, you will need to capture information as quickly as possible. Listen well—behind, between, and beyond the words— and try to get really good at reading body language and sniffing out interests, priorities, and opportunities in the exchange. Being highly emotionally intelligent is a critical requirement for being an excellent negotiator.

3. DETERMINE YOUR STRATEGY AND STYLE FOR THE NEGOTIATION.

Given your goals and priorities, coupled with what you know of the other party, what will it take to persuade them? Negotiations differ, so you have to build a portfolio of strategies to address various situations. For example, if you're asking for a raise, you may decide to make your appeal based on the facts and figures because your boss values these over an emotional appeal (strategy), and you are willing to compromise (style). However, you must recognize that you cannot have just one strategy or style.

Rather than adopting a single style and applying it to every situation, great negotiators carefully assess their situations and develop strategies and tactics accordingly. They understand that context matters. In my example, you may have to become more competitive in your approach as the salary negotiation goes on. Match your strategy and style to fit the specific negotiation situation.

My last recommendation would be to practice as much as possible beforehand, especially if you're nervous about negotiating. Write out what you will say, then practice it until you become comfortable. You can ask a friend to give you feedback, or you can practice in front of a mirror. Also, it is important to negotiate more. The more you negotiate, the better and quicker you will become at it.

CHAPTER 7
FEELING STUCK IN LIFE? HOW TO GET MOVING ... FAST

Do you ever feel like you're stuck in one place and moving forward is impossible? We all go through periods where our work, personal life, or relationships feel stagnant. Implement these five tips into your daily life to get back on track quickly.

1. DO FEWER THINGS

Focus is the key. Set goals and prioritize what is important for you to move ahead. Not prioritizing is the killer of dreams and is equivalent to saying nothing in your life is important. This passage from *Alice in Wonderland* sums it up perfectly.

> "**Alice:** *Would you tell me, please, which way I ought to go from here?*
> **Cheshire Cat:** *That depends a good deal on where you want to get to.*
> **Alice:** *I don't much care where.*
> **Cheshire Cat:** *Then, it doesn't matter which way you go.*"

You're stuck because you don't know where you're going. Set goals, prioritize, and focus. Then, your path will make itself known.

2. FAIL FASTER

When you read the autobiographies of successful people, you will quickly learn that no one escapes failure. These people simply know that the secret to getting ahead is failing. The best failures in life teach you something, so learn from it, and learn fast. Try new things, test out new ideas, and discard the ones that don't work. It's about discovery and using the data and results to get better. Are you stuck? When was the last time you tried something new, tested something out, or learned from a failure?

3. MANAGE YOUR FEAR

Everyone feels fear. People fear failure as much as they fear success. Recognize when you are in the grips of fear—whether it's insecurity, unhealthy thoughts, or anxiety—and have a plan of action for when those feelings hit. People often get stuck in life because, in the grips of fear, they unconsciously react rather than constructively respond. They say no when they should say yes, apply pressure when they should allow for more space, or freeze up when they should act. So figure out how you react when you are fearful and make a plan for how you will respond in the future.

4. WORK ON YOUR EMOTIONAL INTELLIGENCE (EI)

Emotional intelligence, or EI, is the key to getting along with people. One of the biggest causes of failure in the workplace is the inability to get along with others. Knowing what makes you tick and using that information to manage your behavior and work better with others will propel you forward in life. Do you overshare? Do people leave interactions with you feeling down? Are you overly difficult to work with? Get feedback on what you're like from three people who will tell you the truth, then use that information to grow and improve. Working on your EI will give you higher levels of self-awareness, maturity, and self-control.

5. CELEBRATE SMALL WINS

Don't underestimate the boost you can get from recognizing and celebrating your small wins. By default, we tend to focus more on our disapproval and nagging doubts, which sometimes leads us to self-sabotage. Take the time to note your small wins, and pause to focus on what you're learning from failures (#2). Even amidst failure, you will have done something good; take note of your progress.

Put these five tips to practice for one month, and I guarantee you'll see positive results.

CHAPTER 8
HOW TO REALLY LISTEN BETTER TO ENGAGE PEOPLE

> *"When people think you're dying, they really, really listen to you instead of just waiting for their turn to speak."*
>
> —Chuck Palahniuk

Our reality is we live in a world where we have to pay people—coaches, therapists, counselors—to listen to us. This is most likely because humans have a hunger to be listened to, but we live in a time where goldfish[12] have a longer attention span than we do. We miss a lot when we don't actively listen, which is why, to a large degree, effective leadership is effective listening.

The ability to really listen can translate into big wins and can help you become an outstanding boss, employee, or partner. It will increase the trust others place in you, help to significantly reduce conflict, and enable you to better understand how to motivate and gain commitment from the people you work with. Unfortunately, it's not a skill we are taught, nor is it often celebrated in modern society. The visual representation of sharp wit and superior intellect is of a person in action—usually someone who is speaking rather than quietly listening. But listening is just as important, if not more important, than the ability to speak effectively.

HOW DO YOU BECOME A BETTER LISTENER?

I'm going to assume you already know about active listening and its associated techniques, like paraphrasing, asking probing questions, reflecting, and "I" messaging, to name a few. I'm also going to assume you are pretty knowledgeable about the impact of non-verbal communication. You know all of this, yet you still struggle to listen well. What do you do when your mind wanders when you're speaking with someone? How do you deal with people who talk too much or take way too long to make their point? How do you make the people in your life feel heard?

Here are five quick and easy tips to further tune into the people in your life. Practice these, as well as your active listening skills, for the best results.

1. EMOTIONAL MATURITY

There's no getting around emotional maturity; you absolutely need it. Anxiety, stress, discomfort, and defensiveness can impede your willingness to listen. But the ability to listen to someone with an opposing point of view and give them the time to express themselves fully without getting offended or feeling personally attacked is sorely needed now more than ever. We are often socialized to express our opinion. One of the biggest unintended consequences of this is a world saturated with uninformed opinions and an unwillingness to listen and understand other people's points of view. We are invested in winning the argument and often miss the subtle cues that can connect us.

We need emotional maturity to listen better and control our emotions. This control allows us to increase the amount of space between feeling a particular emotion and reacting based upon it. Let's say someone is saying something we don't like or don't want to hear. Rather than reacting instinctively based on how we feel in that moment, we can learn how to observe our feelings, listen with intention, and choose our response more carefully and productively.

This can be difficult at first, but your ability to create that space can improve with practice. Expose yourself to these situations often. Deliberately put yourself in situations where you must listen to people with opposing points of view. Practice pausing before saying or doing anything and choosing the most productive response. This is a critical skill that will help you de-escalate conflicts and find common ground to negotiate.

> *"The single biggest problem in communication is the illusion that it has taken place."*
> —George Bernard Shaw

2. STOP GIVING UNSOLICITED ADVICE

Really, give yourself a break. Sometimes people just want you to hear them out, or they need someone to bounce ideas off of. Perhaps they just want to vent and have their feelings acknowledged. Not everyone needs you to solve their problems or give your opinion. Unless your spouse, colleague, or employee specifically asks for your advice, simply listen and resist the temptation to solve their problem. You can help clarify the issue being discussed or just reflect back to them what you are hearing. This is one of the easiest ways you can make someone feel heard.

3. MAKE OTHERS FEEL HEARD

Making sure people feel heard is significant to the success of your relationships. People will only listen to you when they feel like their opinions and emotions are valued. If you want to make someone feel heard, you have to make them feel as if they have your most valuable commodities—your time and attention. So it's important to create the right environment for the conversation.

- **Timing is critical.** Let people know if it's a bad time for you to listen. Are they trying to talk to you when you're under a deadline? Do you need to leave in five minutes to pick up your kids from school? When necessary, ask to reschedule the conversation for a time when you are more prepared to listen.

- **Move conversations along.** You want to offer your quality time to listen, but this can be abused by people who take forever to make their point or just go on way too long. It's not impolite to stop someone by saying *"Can I tell you what I'm hearing?"* or *"Can I tell you what I've heard so far?"* At that point, you can succinctly summarize the point they are trying to make in an attempt to move the conversation along. If your summary is wrong, then you have not been listening.

- **Listen for others' emotions.** When listening to understand, it's important to also clue in to the speaker's emotions. You pick up much more this way, and it will help keep you focused. Are they annoyed, pleased, frustrated, or anxious? Do their words match the emotions you are hearing? Then, when it's your turn to speak, put a label on it by saying something like, *"You sound annoyed,"* or *"Is this frustrating for you?"*

- **Learn how others want to be listened to.** Does your boss prefer for you to ask questions to show interest? Does your colleague prefer you to quietly nod your head to indicate understanding and not interrupt until he is finished? For the key relationships in your life, take the time to figure out how the person prefers for you to listen, then treat people the way they want to be treated.

- **Remain nonjudgmental.** Communication breaks down when a person feels like they are being judged. In listening mode, you don't have to agree or disagree with anything that's said, and you definitely should not be discounting or shutting down the feelings of others. Avoid phrases, like *"I'm sure things are not that bad,"* or *"That's not how it really is."* These can be demeaning and hurtful.

4. DECIDE TO LISTEN

There's no getting around intention. Without it, your mind will wander because we think at a much faster rate than people speak. Often, people spend time thinking of their response and waiting for their turn to speak. To listen effectively, you have to take a deep breath and make the decision to listen and pay attention. Giving people your attention is the most efficient technique toward quickly building goodwill.

5. PRACTICE FOCUSING YOUR MIND

Immediately take note of when your mind begins to drift during a conversation, then ask the person to repeat what they just said. The aim here is to lengthen your attention span. The problem isn't just your wandering mind, it's that you are often unaware of when it is happening. So be vigilant, and immediately seek to refocus and concentrate. Asking someone to repeat themselves gives you the opportunity to get back into the conversation. If you ask with confidence, your request will most likely be received positively.

The more you practice active listening, the better you will become. Your brain is like a muscle that you must train to stay focused for longer periods. But most importantly, you must stop multitasking because it is so easy to miss subtle cues, which can lead to misunderstandings or hurt feelings. Becoming a better communicator is the one leadership skill that can accelerate your career exponentially. Active listening is the key.

CHAPTER 9
HOW TO CHANNEL ANGER IN A HEALTHY AND POWERFUL WAY

> *"The real art of conversation is not only to say the right thing in the right place, but to leave unsaid the wrong thing at the tempting moment."*
> —Lady Dorothy Nevill

When was the last time you felt truly angry? Everyone gets angry. It's an emotion that's hardwired into the human brain, and sometimes it's justifiable. The phrase "I wouldn't have to manage my anger if people would manage their stupidity" comes to mind here. But whatever you do or say when you're angry can cause more damage in your relationships than the thing that made you angry in the first place. This is because anger is an emotion of action. Research shows that anger[13] is also the most viral emotion, spreading faster than joy and sadness, and can motivate you to do or say things you normally wouldn't. And when you are angry, you tend to not express yourself clearly, making it harder for you to be understood.

I have damaged more relationships than I care to remember

by communicating in anger. Here are three key ways to manage your anger more effectively.

1. You must restrict the expression of your anger to the incident that provoked it. Bringing up anything other than the immediate incident can lead to unfair expressions of anger, which are more likely to damage relationships. Do not spend weeks stewing over unintended slights and quietly simmering, only to explode over one minor issue. Try to address issues and small grievances as they arise, so they do not escalate.

2. How you express yourself is just as important as what you say. Anger is not a good communication tool. The way you speak to people when you are angry is not something that should be taken lightly. Try to lead with kindness. Before responding in anger, take deep breaths to calm your mind, count backward from ten to zero, or ask for a break.

3. Make a distinction between what you are feeling and how you behave. Allow yourself to feel the emotion, but know that just because you *feel* angry doesn't mean you have to *act* angry. While you are taking deep breaths or stepping away from the situation, decide how you'd like to act based on what will be the most helpful and productive at that time.

Applying these tips will allow you to take constructive action, even when you may be feeling out of control.

CHAPTER 10
BOTTOM LINE–HOW TO THRIVE IN A BUREAUCRACY

> *"The simplest way to explain the behavior of any bureaucratic organization is to assume that it is controlled by a cabal of its enemies."*
> —Robert Conquest

If you've ever worked in a bureaucracy or a bureaucratic culture, I know this quote resonates with you in some way. Who hasn't, at some point, looked at the stupefying decisions made by their leaders and thought, *Are they trying to destroy the company?* This quote actually helped me become more patient and less disappointed when confronted with the downside of bureaucracy—the unnecessary complexity, the super slow (or overly quick) decision-making process, and short-term thinking. Bureaucratic cultures can, and often, fail us in many ways, but this quote provided me with the motivation to persist because it can and will get better.

So, is it really possible to thrive in a bureaucracy? And when I say thrive, I don't mean making it to the top of what I like to call "the stink pile," where bad hires, long-term survivors, and hangers-on dwell. Every organization has a stink pile, but in bureaucracies, you will also find some of the greatest people who strive every day to make a difference in the company. This is the tribe you want to connect with, but they are often frustrated and stifled because they refuse to follow the stereotypical bureaucratic, get-ahead recipe of not rocking the boat, going with the flow, and saying yes to every idea that comes from superiors, no matter how dumb, time-wasting, or conflicting they are.

How do you connect with the tribe that's striving to actually make a difference? How do you recognize them? You will often find them engaging in these key practices that are common among great leaders.

1. **They listen hard.** Who can become your strongest supporters in moving ahead? Who can you call on to become your allies in an effort to bring about change? Who should you avoid? When and where are the right opportunities to get your ideas and plans heard? In a bureaucratic culture, great ideas don't always rise to the top or naturally stand out. If you have some, do not think that by speaking up once you will be heard. You have to keep repeating your ideas and proposals for them to be heeded. But knowing when it's the right time, who the key people are to talk to, and how to pitch to them is critical in thriving among this "cabal" of enemies.

2. **They get stronger and more resilient.** This calls for a mindset change. Research[14] by a clinical psychologist, who has been studying resilience for 25 years, shows that one of the key elements of resilience is perception. Do you see your manager's dismissive attitude or constant rejection as a sign to give up sharing? Do you become frustrated when your boss views your input as criticism and takes their frustration out on you? Or do you view your manager's responses as an opportunity to grow and learn how to pitch your ideas better? Your view should be the latter if your intention is to better yourself over time. Don't get stuck feeling unappreciated, ignored, and unmotivated; these feelings are transient. Instead, concentrate on building your skills and becoming more resilient. People who are resilient are more optimistic and emotionally intelligent, and they see failure as a form of helpful feedback. Even after misfortune, resilient people simply change their tactics and soldier on. At some point, you *will* face rejection and failure in your efforts to improve the organization, but don't let that deter you. Keep soldiering on. In bureaucratic cultures, consistent effort, fine-tuned by better listening and connecting with the appropriate tribe, will pay off for you.

3. **They solve problems.** Most bureaucracies tend to focus on the short-term rather than engaging in long-term strategic thinking and planning. Former White House

Chief of Staff Rahm Emanuel was reported to have said, *"Never let a crisis go to waste."* This is very important advice for thriving in a bureaucracy. Most of the fires in these types of cultures are slow-building; everyone can see them coming, but nobody actually does anything about it until the issue blows up into a crisis that can no longer be avoided. Because of this, decisions are often made much quicker. Developing plans of action ahead of time for when issues become full-blown problems will pay great dividends. So this is the perfect time to be heard and get approval for your ideas. Have your proposal and pitch ready for how much it will cost, what the expected outcomes are, and how it will solve the current problem quickly. Perhaps there's a new software you've always wanted the company to buy, or maybe there's a process you think everyone should follow. Whatever your idea is, pitch it as the quickest and easiest solution in the midst of a fire, and you are more likely to get it approved. You will become known as someone who is great at solving immediate problems, and this will enhance your authority and credibility.

My experience shows that these are the three most actionable ways to thrive in a bureaucracy. However, if you have reached the point in your career where you dread going into work every day and cannot endure one more reactive change, then my final tip is to get out now. No, seriously, I mean it. Bureaucratic cultures are not for everyone, and if you don't know how to navigate them, you will end up surrounded by people in the stink pile. The saying "If you lie down with dogs, you will get up with fleas" applies here. Hanging with the stink pile will cause you to become a flea-ridden mess, i.e. disgruntled and checked out. More critically, getting rid of fleas is hard and often comes with secondary bouts of fear, incompetence, insecurity, and dysfunctional behavior. After a while in this type of unsatisfactory environment, your definition of success will start to morph into a singular "Did I make it through the day?" rather than a collective "Have we accomplished what we needed to today?"

I believe great employees can and do thrive in bureaucratic cultures; they just have to want it for themselves.

Questions to Ponder

"Many of us choose security over freedom to such an extreme that we confine ourselves and profoundly limit our experience of life. I might surrender to a craving to be secure by electing to live out my life in a box. Maximum safety, minimum existence."
—Gordon MacKenzie

Am I living in a box for maximum safety? Where do I need to empower myself? What powers do I need to wake up and unleash? What's the one thing I can do right now to shift my life?

_____

_____

_____

_____

_____

_____

_____

_____

_____

_____

_____

SECTION 3
ROAR

"Did you think the lion was sleeping because he did not roar?"

—Friedrich Schiller

CHAPTER 11
MINDFUL? OR IS YOUR MIND UNUSUALLY FULL

> *"People think not knowing is being lost. In that moment of being lost, stay in the unknowing; it will come. It always comes. It's a process. People are always looking for events. We're a very event-oriented culture. People have no room for process. It's because they are too anxious. You have to sit with your anxiety, five minutes a day, sit."*
>
> —Abdi Assadi

Being a leader in this modern world comes with a lot of anxiety. The digital lifestyle we live in can be complicated, cluttered, and volatile. We have large amounts of data coming at us constantly—e-mails, voicemails, requests, and decisions that need to be made quickly. In addition, our workload has become increasingly complex, and we are often accessible twenty-four seven, which brings with it a sense of urgency and importance that's tough to resist. But even more troubling, people who are responsive to these communications are considered to be more effective. Think about this for a minute. If you frequently send an email to two people and one consistently responds within twenty-four hours, who will you believe is more competent? The problem is we cannot keep up with this pace. Burnout often results.

This is where the practice of being mindful becomes helpful and necessary. Rather than running the rat race, mindful awareness is as Psychotherapist Donald Altman says, "a way of being that asks us to pay attention, be curious, and intentional in our lives." Mindfulness is a very old technique that is becoming increasingly popular in today's world. People use mindfulness to reduce stress and gain a greater sense of control in their lives. It changes how you use your attention and awareness and helps you become more adaptive. Mindfulness helps people get more enjoyment out of their good times and handle their bad times better.

Where this concept really connects in terms of leadership is in what we know about emotional intelligence. Mindfulness enhances emotional intelligence, notably self-awareness and the capacity to manage distressing emotions. Emotions are contagious. If you're feeling overwhelmed or stressed out, the people around you pick up on those emotions, and it affects them. As leaders, we need to monitor our moods through self-awareness, change them for the better through self-management, and act in ways that improve the relationships we have with our employees and colleagues. Practicing mindfulness helps with this. It is foundational to the practice of great leadership and helps integrate various leadership competencies and skills.

How can you practice mindful awareness quickly and easily in your daily life? Here are a few tips:

1. Focus on one task at a time; don't multitask. When you're driving, just drive; don't try to text or talk at the same time. Like the popular Zen proverb says, *"When walking, walk. When eating, eat."*

2. Eat your lunch slowly and savor your food. Stop eating while you're hunched over your desk doing work.

3. Practice meditation. Either begin or end your day with a few minutes of a quiet, contemplative practice.

4. Be present in all of your conversations. Really listen to the person instead of just thinking about what you want to say next. Enjoy your time with them. In addition, engage in fewer conversations with people you don't enjoy speaking to. This will allow you to have more energy for those you actually like.

5. Do less. Everyone's busy, but busy doing what? Try to cut unimportant tasks from your day and only focus on what's truly important. What are your priorities? What's on your "not to-do" list.

6. Do nothing for five minutes a day. Focus on your breathing, sit in silence, and notice the world around you. As Assadi suggested, try to sit with your anxiety for five minutes a day. It's good for you.

7. Create mindfulness triggers. Pick a few tasks you do every day, and be mindful and aware of when you are

doing them. For example, before entering your office in the morning, remind yourself of your purpose and recommit to your vision as a leader.

Hopefully, these little steps can help you enjoy the journey of life more with less unnecessary stress.

CHAPTER 12
ACTUALLY, THIS IS WHY YOU'RE NOT AT PEAK PRODUCTIVITY

One of the top challenges we face every day is figuring out how to fit everything we need to do into the time we have available. Every one of us has experienced that moment of dread when we feel we are not going to get everything done on time. I have spent a lot of time over the years poring over the latest productivity research, videos, books, and articles to give my clients the best information to make them more productive. This research has shaped my views on time management and productivity issues and has helped me identify the six key mistakes we all make that impede our productivity.

MISTAKE #1: AN INABILITY TO SAY NO

In other words, this is an inability to prioritize. Learn how to say no to anything that is not a priority. This has the biggest impact on your ability to focus on what is most important for accomplishing your goals. Master this, and you will find that your day opens up and you have more free time to work on your priorities. At work, you determine your priorities by detailing the tasks where your performance will be judged, e.g. the projects that advance the overall goals of your organization.

MISTAKE #2: YOU ARE BUSY BUT NOT PRODUCTIVE

You're busy with the urgency of day-to-day life, but goals for moving the organization and your career forward often go untended. Activities that keep you busy tend to be e-mails, meetings, presentations, document preparation, and planning. Examples of some company goals include increasing sales by 20% by the end of the quarter or increasing customer satisfaction scores by five points by the end of the year. Both categories are necessary, but when it comes to peak productivity, you have to adopt the right mindset. Just because you answered 200 emails, made a presentation, prepared a report, attended four meetings, and engaged in eight phone calls doesn't mean you were productive. If 60% of those activities had nothing to do with advancing your goals, then you were busy for virtually no reason.

MISTAKE #3: YOU MULTITASK DURING MEETINGS

If you ever find yourself multitasking during meetings or conference calls, you are likely wasting your time by attending meetings you should not be in. If your focus and attention is not required, then your presence is not needed. You are not being productive, so learn how to say no to these types of meetings. In addition, multitasking kills your focus. Research shows that even though we feel like we are getting more done, it actually makes us less efficient. So, while multitasking may make you feel emotionally satisfied, it actually decreases your productivity over time.

MISTAKE #4: YOUR HEALTH HABITS DON'T SUPPORT YOUR GOALS

Your body is an amazing machine, but without the proper support, it will fail. In 2012, the Centers for Disease Control and Prevention stated that physical inactivity[15] may be the most major risk factor for cancer for non-smoking individuals. Perform an energy audit on yourself; do you eat right, work out regularly, and get enough sleep? If you don't do these things, you will not be productive for very long. You need to manage your energy, so you can work hard and feel good while doing it, which will allow you to effectively manage your time in the process.

MISTAKE #5: YOU WRITE A TO-DO LIST

To-do lists are not enough to increase your productivity. Don't get me wrong, though, to-do lists are great as a first step in getting rid of that overwhelming feeling we all experience. Research shows that writing things down reduces worry and organizes our thoughts. But you must go beyond this step to become highly productive. Put your to-dos on your calendar and assign a specific time to each task. Until it has been put on your calendar, your to-do list is really just a lot of hopeful thinking. Becoming overly optimistic about the time we have to complete a task often limits our productivity in the long run. We think we can get more done when, in reality, our time is limited. Placing realistically timed tasks on your calendar helps you avoid this mistake.

MISTAKE #6: YOU DON'T MANAGE YOUR MOOD

You cannot be frazzled on the inside and organized externally at the same time. It is easier to focus on your priorities if you set yourself up to start the day in a calm and peaceful way. If you start the day frazzled—sporadically checking emails with people pulling you in all directions—you will be in a reactive mode the entire day, and other people will determine your priorities for you. Research[16] shows that if you start the day in a calm way, you are more likely to focus and get the right things done. Start the day off with some meditation or exercise to calm your mind, reduce stress, and improve your ability to stay focused.

When asked what she does first thing in the morning, Dr. Velma Scantlebury, associate chief of Transplant Surgery at Christian Care Health System in Delaware, said,[17] *"I meditate if I'm not waking up with a donor kidney on the way."* Dr. Scantlebury has performed over 1,000 kidney transplants in her career. If she can find the time to meditate and calm her mind in the morning, so can we. And unlike her, we don't always have to choose between meditation and saving someone's life.

In a world where we're faced with large amounts of data and a constant stream of e-mails, voicemails, and text messages, it can often feel chaotic. To be productive, we must cling to our priorities, make peace with the tasks we must place on the back burner, and be ruthless in working to avoid these six mistakes.

CHAPTER 13
HOW TO DEAL WITH THE MESSY MIDDLE—PRACTICAL ADVICE

You'll encounter messy moments along your journey, particularly when you are in the midst of a change or transition. Feeling uncomfortable, dissatisfied, or discouraged is a normal, and sometimes necessary part of taking on a new work project, a new position, or a major goal for your personal growth and development. You start out feeling great, fired up with enthusiasm and energy, then you stumble squarely into the middle of what often seems like a big, complex, confusing mess. Sound familiar? Welcome to the messy middle.

How do you navigate this? How do you revitalize your drive and enthusiasm to get to the finish line? What do successful people know that we don't? Successful people know how to effectively handle the messy middle in moments of transition. They know there is grit in the oyster before the pearl. They don't mistake progress for a mess, and they understand that the messy middle is normal during times of change and transition and often comes with feelings of anxiety and fear.

To achieve your goals, you have to figure out how to manage

the fear and anxiety that come with the messy middle. If you don't, you will get discouraged and set yourself up for failure when you reach this pivotal moment.

So, what are some ways you can manage the fear and anxiety of the messy middle? Here are some of my suggestions.

1. Always try to operate from the perspective of *How much progress am I making toward my goal?* Are you inching closer? Change happens in incremental steps. You can get through the messy middle by breaking your project into bite-size pieces and working on them one step at a time. Regularly check your progress, so you can recognize when you're moving forward. It doesn't matter how small the result is. You have to intentionally look for the progress amidst the mess.

2. Write an "already done" list with the tasks you've already completed on your path toward your goal and vision. These little successes will help you stay positive and keep you motivated.

3. Stop comparing yourself to other people. There is a lot of empirical research[18] backing up the saying "Comparison is the thief of joy." Comparing yourself to others is deflating, and during the messy middle, you want to keep yourself motivated to act and think appropriately.

4. Challenge your worrisome thoughts by reminding yourself of your strengths. During the messy middle, things may go wrong. Now is the time to examine how you can use your strengths to handle the situation. Are you a good listener? Are you good at sharing your opinions? Play to your strengths and actively use them to problem solve.

5. Visualize your success. There is power in visualization. Great athletes, like Muhammad Ali and Michael Jordan, used this tool to envision their success before it even happened. This mindset shift can drastically alter your beliefs and perceptions about a situation, leading to a greater chance of forward progress.

6. Stop resenting the struggle long enough to see what the struggle is revealing about you. Every storm is your servant; it teaches you something about yourself. Look for the lesson in the messy middle. What is being shown to you? Is this struggle going to reveal a strength you never knew you had?

Always remember that success is born in the messy middle. Embrace the challenges and let them shape you into the person you are meant to be.

Questions to Ponder

"If we do what is necessary, all the odds are in our favor."

—Henry Kissinger,
Former U.S. Secretary of State

Ask yourself the following questions: What is necessary today? Am I doing it? If not, why not? What are my big-picture goals? How am I moving toward them?

_____

_____

_____

_____

_____

_____

_____

_____

_____

_____

_____

_____

_____

_____

SECTION 4
LEADING A COMPANY TO SUCCESS

"The goal is to win, not to look like you're winning."
—Anonymous

FOR LEADERS, PRECISION MATTERS

As a leader assigning high-priority projects to key staff, collaborators, suppliers, or contractors, you should first figure out what aspects of the project you—and only you as the leader—can get done.

If you don't figure this out, your time allocations will be wrong, and you will become a bottleneck, preventing work from moving forward because you cannot handle the pace and number of requests that land on your desk, potentially becoming single points of failure for the company. As your work and business grows, you will find yourself relying more on others to accomplish goals. Delegating tasks is perfectly OK; you cannot do everything alone. But when determining where to spend your time, precision matters.

CHAPTER 14
HOW TO LEAD IN AN UNCERTAIN WORLD

"Fortune favors the prepared mind."
—Louis Pasteur

We all live with some level of uncertainty. In my work, I see it reflected in my two specialty areas as a change manager and a learning and development specialist. As a change manager, I see leaders engaged in the daily battle to stay competitive. Core businesses are under threat, primarily due to fluctuating consumer behaviors, market conditions, and technological advancements that require leaders to revisit their operational strategies often. This battle to triumph, to figure out what is next, is best described by business advisor Ram Charan as "perceptual acuity," or the ability to sense what is coming before the fog clears. Those leaders who get it right figure out what changes are needed to position their organizations to capture robust growth. After all, organizational success today is built on finding and exploiting new market opportunities and increasing revenues. Thriving organizations do not budget cut their way to greatness.

As a learning and development specialist, I see this uncertainty reflected in the questions of employees. *How do I move past the fear of failing? How do I move forward when I'm not sure of my place in this new dispensation?* Employees often struggle with the anxiety and fear that accompany the demands of organizational changes, and as a result, uncertainty becomes the new normal.

As a leader, we are usually recognized for being decisive and knowledgeable. But what do you do when there appears to be no right answer to the challenges confronting your organization, when you are overwhelmed by your company's circumstances? Acknowledging uncertainty or telling an employee *"I do not know"* can be difficult for some leaders, but this is what uncertainty brings to the table. In today's complex environments, where there is no hope for certainty, how do you lead when you are not sure what's coming next?

HIDDEN IN PLAIN SIGHT: PAY ATTENTION

The first question to ask amid uncertainty is *"Have you been paying attention?"* For most companies, the challenge isn't just the uncertain times but whether leaders have built the capability within their organizations to pick up on future industry changes. Leaders must hone in on this capability, so they can respond, plan, and prepare the organization to discover and exploit new growth opportunities. Most organizations are so busy with the tasks associated with just keeping the doors open that their leaders do not pay attention and miss the signposts and signals along the way.

Let's examine some well-known companies to illustrate this. Digital books and music did not destroy Borders; it was the Borders team's inability to note the shift toward digital products and create a strategy for this scenario. Similarly, online streaming did not shut down Blockbuster; it was the company's inability to recognize the coming shift and prepare its operations to exploit it. In both cases, it was not the disruptive technology that destroyed the company; it was its leaders' inability to recognize and plan for a future scenario where that technology was dominant. The leaders simply did not pay attention. New markets, underserved markets, or new ways to deliver on a mission are missed when leaders do not pay attention.

On the other hand, let's look at Nokia Oyj. Once upon a time, it was the leading vendor in smartphones, then it lost its crown to Apple and Samsung. However, in 2014, its incoming CEO aggressively moved the company into areas like equipment and services to capture new growth. Since selling its smartphone business to Microsoft, Nokia has successfully transferred its core business to networking equipment for mobile carriers, where it is currently outperforming its competitors and defying industry trends.

Even Microsoft, once the vanguard of consumer technology, has managed to thrive and capture new growth. Its core business is now enterprise and cloud software, which was a strategy that was actively pursued by Satya Nadella, the company's CEO, when he arrived in 2014. Nadella recently noted in an interview,[19] *"No status quo in any part of Microsoft's organization should be counted on."* Today, we think of Apple, not Microsoft, when we talk about the "cool factor" as it relates to the consumer market. But with this shift, Microsoft's CEO has ensured that Apple's star quality no longer affects Microsoft's bottom line.

What did these two companies have that the previous two did not? They had leaders who knew how to plan for uncertainty and knew when to switch up their core business, company visions, and strategies to capture new, highly applicable growth across a range of futures.

IMPROVE FORESIGHT TO FACILITATE DECISION MAKING DURING UNCERTAIN TIMES

Organizational leaders can only say *"We do not know"* for a limited time before employees start to become disengaged and disconnected. When the way forward is not clear, can change at will, or is muddied with a variety of options, organizational leaders must improve their predictive skills, so a framework for critical decisions can be established. Leaders must utilize the information gleaned from paying attention to consider the future and envision a range of possible future scenarios. What's around the corner for their market and industry? What are the trends that signal new opportunities for their organization? What will be the impact? Which possible scenarios will they need to prepare strategies for? In other words, building upon your strategic planning process is essential in this new norm, enabling organizations to develop a variety of scenarios and strategies for an uncertain future. This is preferable to waiting around for whatever your market/industry throws at you. Fortune favors the prepared mind.

TIPS FOR UPGRADING YOUR STRATEGIC PLANNING PROCESS

Every leader should build upon their strategic planning process to allow for some foresight planning. Here are some basic tips to get started.

1. Assemble a team of employees to generate possible futures for the organization. Ask questions and get multiple perspectives from a wide range of people, like the leadership team, employees who are knowledgeable about the industry and are likely to see and recognize trends that can be exploited, or people you normally don't listen to or learn from. Tap into their knowledge and utilize it as necessary.

2. Collate any ideas, trends, and scenarios and see if they can be grouped into different themes or patterns. Connect the observations and insights to possible scenarios and actions.

3. Select the optimal scenarios from these patterns, flesh them out, then examine the consequences for the organization's various stakeholders.

4. Based on this analysis, select the pertinent and possible future scenarios for the organization and determine the possible outcomes.

5. Develop strategies, possible action plans, strategic messaging, and so on for each scenario to achieve the stated outcomes.

6. From these scenarios and strategies, create a vision map of the future that points the way forward and allows leaders to engage their internal and external stakeholders as your situation changes.

7. Test your current vision against the future scenarios. Is it applicable across the range of possible future scenarios?

This is not traditional strategic planning as we know it, which is rooted in selecting the singular path forward and developing strategies to get there. This type of planning requires a more flexible and continuous process, one that includes foresight and produces a framework for leaders to make dynamic decisions during times of uncertainty.

WE ARE NOT ORACLES

"The only thing I cannot predict is the future."
—Amit Trivedi

It is important to end with an acknowledgement of the

obvious: No one can predict the future with 100% accuracy, and no amplified strategic planning process can, with full accuracy, calculate and account for all the variables in our highly complex world. Yes, it is hard, and yes, it is easy to get this wrong. Still, this does not mean leaders should not work on building this capability, as it is necessary for survival. In a 2015 memo[20] sent to employees, Microsoft's CEO wrote, *"We need to be always learning and insatiably curious. We need to be willing to lean into uncertainty, take risks and move quickly when we make mistakes, recognizing failure happens along the way to mastery."* This is the mindset that sees opportunity in uncertainty.

CHAPTER 15
HOW TO HARNESS ORGANIZATIONAL CHAOS DURING TRANSITIONS

"It was an organization in complete, unrelenting chaos." These were the words Susan Fowler used to describe her time working at Uber.[21] While many of us do not work for an aggressively growing start-up, we can still identify with the feeling of complete chaos at work. For most people, change is usually the culprit for a chaotic work environment, and in a lot of these cases, it generally starts with the appointment of a new leader. Recently, during a conference presentation on change, I gave a snapshot of an employee resisting change, and 70% of the managers in the room said it was a snapshot of their current situation. If you know anything about successfully implementing change in an organization, you will understand that having resistant middle managers, the people charged with executing the goals and strategies, is not the pathway to success. Upon further analysis, I was not surprised to discover that many were dealing with new bosses. Change your leader, and you change your world.

To push the organization toward bigger and better results,

new leaders must walk a tightrope between ensuring the organization maintains what's going well and disrupting the behaviors and thinking behind what is going wrong. New leaders often come in energetic, engaged, and driven to succeed, bringing new ideas, systems, and approaches. But if not managed well, what new leaders see as a needed reset of strategic focus to address market forces, employees perceive as chaos. We all know the signs: unclear direction, competing priorities, impossible deadlines, a tendency to hop from project to project or strategy to strategy—all with a frenetic vibe that is exhausting for everyone involved.

Most employees prefer the solid reassurance of certainty over the turmoil and stress caused by new ideas and approaches. Change disrupts certainty, and our brains are wired to seek rewards and avoid threats. The changes of a new leader are often viewed as a threat to the solid, safe, and predictable ground employees are accustomed to standing on. The latest organizational research by Pfeffer & Hardisty[22] also reveals that the more uncertain people are, the less likely they are to take risks. The irony here, of course, is that when implementing changes, this is exactly what new leaders need from their team—for them to step out of their comfort zones and take a risk. But quite often, asking employees to take on that mindset can come across like advising someone who has experienced substantial losses in an investment to "double down" and throw the remaining few dollars they have into the failing investment in hopes it will pay off. Most people are risk- and loss-averse.

So, beneath the chaos of change, a new leader must provide

just enough solid ground to keep employees productive. Here are three specific approaches to help employees embrace the unstable, challenging, and sometimes chaotic nature of transitions.

1. COUNTERBALANCE NEW CHANGES WITH TRAINING

Ultimately, every new leader must deal with an organization filled with employees who lack the agility to quickly adapt. They find themselves developing new strategies and tactics much faster than employees can adopt them. The key to convincing employees to keep their focus on identifying and exploiting opportunities in a dynamic environment lies in the provision of ongoing training. New leaders must dedicate the resources needed to provide employees with monthly training to reduce the accompanying fear, uncertainty, and resistance associated with change. These trainings help employees develop the mindset and skills needed to become more agile and flexible. The key skills I recommend focusing on are those that encourage faster decision-making, better team synergy, and a bias toward action, like Decision-Making as a Competitive Advantage, How to Navigate Change, Teamwork: Increasing Social Psychology, Execution: Translating Goals into Action, Advanced Communication (e.g. How to be Constructively Candid), etc.

Organizations have always strived for efficiency and stability, but developing agility does not happen organically; new leaders must make it happen. Do not underestimate the amount of training needed around increasing agility to reduce organizational chaos.

2. REINFORCE YOUR VISION AND YOUR "WHY" TO GIVE CLEAR DECISION-MAKING CRITERIA

Central to reducing chaos is ensuring employees are empowered to make decisions and act as the leader would when he/she is not present. In my years of consulting experience, I cannot emphasize enough just how often employees report a delay in progress because timely decisions are not made. New leaders must ensure every employee understands their vision of the future and why things must change. Purpose matters, and it must meaningfully inform decisions to help employees move forward through the discomfort and uncertainty of transition.

Without some solid criteria from which employees can quickly make decisions, chaos is inevitable. If you are getting resistance (passive or active) as a new leader, choose to take it as clear feedback that your vision is not resonating and people are not buying into your "why," the reason you are making them change.

This may mean more work for you and the leadership team, but it's crucial that you get out there, listen to people's fears and concerns, become more visible in communicating the vision and the "why" of the change, figure out and remove the stumbling blocks holding people back, convey and act on the lessons learned along the way, and create more opportunities for employee collaboration and contribution. Without these actions, ambiguity will rule, decisions will not be made in a timely fashion, and politics and self-interest will start to dictate what happens during the change.

3. BUILD CAPACITY BY BREAKING DOWN SILOS

Operational silos delay decisions, weaken collaboration, and limit an organization's ability to quickly adapt to change. New leaders need to create a process and foster a culture that allows people in different functions and at different levels in the organization to work together to move their agenda forward. The form that this takes is left up to the leader (e.g. a meeting, forum, etc.), but new leaders must regularly bring all managers together in the same room to solve problems and facilitate quicker decision-making that is unconstrained by turfs, functions, levels, and/or politics. This will increase the capacity of the organization to limit chaos while taking advantage of new opportunities and executing on strategies and goals. Again, this does not happen organically, and the new leader must organize a way for this to occur frequently. The executive team should not be the only ones meeting regularly.

How do you know if you need to build capacity in your organization? If a project/change has ever been slowed or has failed for one of the following reasons, you need to build capacity:

1. A lengthy review and sign-off process grinded to a halt in one department;

2. The wrong stakeholder and/or department ended up making critical decisions that negatively impacted the project;

3. There was a duplication of work, and contradictory decisions were made that slowed the project;

4. Key people felt excluded from conversations around the project and didn't make needed input in a timely manner; or

5. The project came in over budget and/or behind schedule.

Building capacity by breaking down silos, i.e. getting everyone working on the same problem, is the fastest way new leaders can create alignment on the same priorities, build team cohesiveness, shorten the decision-making process, and bring about change.

> *"All great changes are preceded by chaos."*
> —Deepak Chopra

Finally, we live in a fast-paced and uncertain environment, and while chaos can be contained and harnessed, it cannot be eliminated. Organizations today should always be prepared to change directions. We should all be familiar with the saying "Make yourself at home, but don't get too comfortable." Expecting to make necessary adjustments and changes without experiencing some form of chaos before and during the process is a faulty mindset. This may sound paradoxical, but it is not. A franchise owner who is opening a new store will have some chaos closer to opening time. For a person undergoing certification testing, the period just before the exam can feel chaotic. You can contain it by preparing well for the store opening and the exam, but that little bit of chaos adds to the eventual success. Disorder often results when you try new things, so it's imperative that employees (through training, communication, and coaching) understand that growth cannot happen without it. A leader's job is to ensure the chaos is temporary and limited to only periods of growth and improvement.

CHAPTER 16
HOW TO GIVE FEEDBACK THAT GETS RESULTS WITHOUT CONFLICT

We all have to give feedback, whether it be to an intern, an employee, a child, or a spouse. When people make mistakes, it's up to us, as leaders, to give feedback. Here's a key tip when doing so: Ensure you're giving feedback and not just criticizing someone.

What's the difference? Criticism invalidates a person, offering nothing beyond *"You have done something wrong"* or *"You are wrong."* It makes the person feel badly about themselves or look foolish. Feedback, on the other hand, is about acknowledging what's good and how it can be better. It's constructive, which makes it a two-way conversation. We respond differently to criticism than we do feedback because the feedback process allows for different ways of doing things and seeking the best solution for everyone involved.

I used to be lousy at giving feedback but was quite practiced at offering criticism. It took me a while to figure out how to give feedback without alienating or offending the other party or having the exchange devolve into discomforting conflict. Have you ever found yourself procrastinating in giving feedback because you feared the other person would get defensive and begin to argue with you? Have you ever tried giving feedback, persisting through the discomfort, only for nothing to change? Allow me to share a major lesson I have learned from my painful stumbles.

THE SECRET: BUILD GOODWILL LONG BEFORE YOU NEED TO GIVE CONSTRUCTIVE FEEDBACK

I don't think anyone needs guidance on how to give feedback to someone who has done a great job. The biggest mistake leaders make today in giving feedback is not praising people often enough. We get caught up in the daily routine of life and do not see the need to praise someone for doing what they're being paid to do. I have heard the phrase "Get your praise at home" used to justify the lack of recognition for those employees who are creating value in their organizations. Some leaders prefer employees be motivated by what they accomplish at work and how much money they are paid rather than noticing and giving praise when necessary. But research[23] consistently shows that employees who feel valued at work are more engaged, and that often begins with recognition and feedback.

I believe we should constantly strive to recognize and praise people who do good work for two reasons. First, people repeat the behaviors they are praised for, and second, it is the quickest and easiest way to build trust and credibility with someone, which are essential components when you have to give constructive feedback. Research[24] also shows we're wired to remember the bad things people say to us. By taking a couple minutes each week to let an employee or a colleague know you see the good work they are doing, you're creating an environment for that behavior to continue, and you are building up goodwill you can then draw on later to smooth the process of giving feedback. Telling someone they need to redo work, improve, or stop a certain action will not resonate until that person believes you have their best interests at heart.

Credibility and trust are the key ingredients when giving feedback to others. Without it, defensiveness, resistance, or disruptive conflicts can result. When giving feedback, the person must feel that you see them in their entirety—the things they do well, as well as the things they can do to improve. Start acknowledging the good things people are doing within your organization. It is not a waste of your time; it's an *investment* of your time. Some examples of these one-minute investments include:

> "Sarah, you always get the right tone with difficult customers."
> "Richard, yet again, I was able to rely on you this week to get the report in on time."
> "Daniel, I really like how you answer the phone so promptly and professionally."
> "Cara, I appreciate your respect for company time. You always arrive so promptly."

Once, you have cleared the hurdle of building trust and credibility with the people in your organization, the steps to give constructive and effective feedback are easy to follow.

1. Ask for permission to give feedback.
2. Be specific about any concerns you may have.
3. Explain the impact of those concerns.
4. Pause and ask for the other person's perspective.
5. Note where you agree and differ.
6. Come up with solutions together.
7. Listen hard and follow up.

Let's imagine one of your key employees, Sarah, is submitting a project proposal (Lakewood proposal) for your review. After your review, you will present the proposal to your senior management team; however, the proposal is now two days late, and Sarah has not spoken to you about it. How do you go about giving feedback?

1. **Ask for permission to give feedback.** By doing so, you also acknowledge the need for feedback in a timely manner. "Hi, Sarah. I was expecting the Lakewood proposal two days ago as agreed. Can we meet to talk about it?"

2. In a feedback meeting, **be specific about your concerns**. Now is not the time to be vague. Restrict your feedback to things you know for certain and not what you think or might have heard. Again, you are focusing

on description rather than judgement. *"You missed the deadline we agreed to"* is preferred over *"You're being irresponsible and unfair to me. You're always missing deadlines."*

3. **Explain the impact of your concerns.** Begin your sentences with *"When you..."* and *"I feel..."* to get your point across. *"When you miss a deadline like this, I feel frustrated because it limits the time I need to review and make any adjustments before I present it. And as far as I can tell, you didn't let me know you would be late or that you needed more time. I feel out-of-the-loop when this happens, and it worries me."*

4. **Pause and ask for the other person's perspective.** This allows for a two-way discussion that helps clarify expectations and outcomes. *"What do you think?"* or *"How are you viewing this situation?"* are great ways to approach this scenario.

5. **Note where you agree and differ.** Recognizing the areas where you agree will help build a sense of common ground that will allow you to better tackle where you differ. *"Sarah, I agree that your attention to detail is incredibly important, and it is what helps you do such a great job. Your perfectionism definitely aids you here, but this is where we differ. I can see that it is also hurting you in a critical area—getting things in on time. Let's explore*

why you feel that timeliness is secondary in a situation such as this."

6. **Come up with solutions together** to avoid this situation in the future and get the outcome you are looking for. Do not get caught up in specific procedures or processes. Simply agree on outcomes by first stating what you want. *"I would prefer to be updated if you think you will miss a deadline. That way, I can lend any support that is needed. What's your idea to avoid this in the future?"* Then, you could say, *"I would like you to manage your perfectionism better to avoid missing deadlines in the future. Your work is too good to be derailed by missed deadlines. Do you have any ideas you want to share on how you can manage this?"*

7. Then, **listen hard for their feedback** and alternatives. Let people solve their own problems, then hold them accountable for any agreements. *"We've agreed that you will… I think we understand each other better after this discussion. I will take your priorities under consideration when establishing deadlines, and I'll expect you to come straight to me if any deadlines become a problem."*

Remember to respect the person you are dealing with. Effective feedback is about expressing how you feel, offering a suggestion for how it can be improved, and demonstrating that you're willing to listen to the other person's perspective and solutions. Everyone sees and responds to situations differently.

Feedback recognizes there are different ways of doing things, and we want the best solution for everyone involved. Think win-win when interacting with people. You want to be able to express dissatisfaction, concern, or confusion without disrupting your relationships.

This is a critical leadership skill. Along with being a great listener, these skills will markedly improve your ability to get along with people, which is something former President Theodore Roosevelt referred to as "the most important single ingredient in the formula to success."

CHAPTER 17
THIS WILL MAKE YOU A CLEAR COMMUNICATOR

In her book *SmartTribes: How Teams Become Brilliant Together*,[25] Christine Comaford puts a spotlight on the need for clarity when leaders are communicating. Saying what we truly mean and expressing what we truly need requires us to engage in communication that is more explicit, limiting our implicit communication and expectations. Explicit expectations are stated outright; we know exactly what is expected of us in detail. For example, my manager might say, *"Please send me a spreadsheet of our marketing activities for the year by Monday, June 30. Thanks."*

Implicit expectations, on the other hand, are those we think people should know or figure out. So, in this example, implicit information could include what time on June 30th, which file format (email/hard copy), what context, or any additional details you need to get the job done correctly the first time.

The only way your team will know what you mean is if you explicitly tell them. Vague information often leads to confusion and opens the door for misinterpretation and distrust. The first key in communication is to be as explicit as possible by stating your expectations clearly and requesting others do the same. If the manager in the above example wanted to be more explicit, they might say, *"Please email me a spreadsheet of our marketing activities, the expenses associated with these activities, and how much money we have left in the budget for the year. I will need it by the end of the day on Monday, June 30. Thanks."*

If you are not getting the results you want from your interactions with other people, you should ask yourself, *Am I making clear requests? Am I being explicit enough? Do I have implicit intentions or expectations I am not articulating?* If people often say to you, *"I didn't know that"* during projects, take heed and be more explicit with your intentions and expectations.

CHAPTER 18
THIS IS WHY GREAT LEADERS FOCUS ON CUSTOMER SERVICE

One of my more popular training requests is for customer service. I see it as an essential area leaders should be focused on. How can you and your team become better at improving your customers' experiences?

Research shows that customer service *drives* revenue growth.

- 86% of customers are willing to pay more for a better customer experience.[26]
- A 5% increase in customer retention increases profit by 25% to 95%.[27]
- Companies that prioritize the customer experience generate 60% higher profits than their competitors.[28]

Neglect this area, and your business and career will suffer, no matter how great of a leader you are. To start improving your customer service today, ask yourself a few simple questions.

1. **What is great customer service to you?** It's common sense, but defining it helps you paint a vision and make it common practice.

2. **Who is your customer?** Your customers can be internal, external, direct, or indirect. For example, if you run a bakery, your customer is not only the person buying your birthday cake (direct) but the family member they gift the cake to (indirect). Know who you are serving and determine if you want to treat them all the same.

3. **What are your service characteristics?** It's important to understand your customers' expectations, then deliver on them accordingly. It is also important to ensure you have systems in place that support your customer and your employees are trained and empowered to deliver consistently. Neglecting to design and implement systems and processes that support your customer service standards is where most leaders fail.

4. **How do you think your customers see you?** Would your customers agree that you are meeting their expectations?

5. **What does your "moment of truth" say about your business?** A moment of truth is defined as "any episode in which a customer comes into contact with any aspect of the organization and gets an impression of the

quality of service".[29] Good customer service is all about improving the moment of truth.

Knowing the answers to these questions will get you started on prioritizing your customers' experiences.

CHAPTER 19
HOW TO BECOME A MORE AWESOME LEADER

Becoming a better leader is mostly done through experience, trial and error, and reflection, beginning with a leader philosophy that guides your actions and decisions. In this way, you're aware of how you want to approach the common practices of leadership and whether your preferred style fits with your current organization and situation.

Once you've gotten comfortable with your philosophy, living it does not happen overnight. It's a continuous, dynamic process, and the most important thing you need to do is develop a feedback process that helps you figure out if you're fulfilling it. This is where learning to lead through experience, trial and error, and reflection comes into play.

Truly successful leaders welcome feedback that helps them learn, grow, and become more self-aware. This does not happen organically; it is something you must be deliberate about. The reason so many leaders fail is because they don't develop a process that enables them to capture and critically use feedback. Competitiveness, the need to be right, and denial are often the biggest hurdles leaders face in becoming self-aware. Without feedback that enables you to understand how you're performing and functioning as a leader, you cannot improve, so you must focus intently on developing a feedback process. I've listed three steps below that can help.

1. **Listen hard**. Listen to the off-the-cuff, casual remarks people make about you and write them down. Pretty soon, you will know how you are coming across to others. Compare these comments to the words or phrases you use to describe how you want to lead. Do people see you as you wish to be seen? If not, your actions are not following your philosophy. You also need to pay attention to whether or not your philosophy is valued or needed. Spend time listening and building channels of communication where you can get feedback from a variety of people.

2. **Ask for feedback**. Ask an honest friend or colleague how you're performing in the workplace. Instead of asking, *"How do you think I'm doing?"* ask *"How can I be a better leader/team member/colleague?"* You don't need to be excessive about it, but it is important to ask these questions. For example, if you think you are flexible and approachable, but others say you're not, then you will know you need to work on that area.

3. **Connect**. Take complete responsibility for how you are heard. Effective communication is a fine art, so work on improving it. Figure out how you can get your message

across better. Sometimes your philosophy may not be the problem, but your communication style is.

Creating a feedback process you can learn from and reflect on is the key to improving your leadership skills. Finally, recognize that your leadership puzzle is never completely finished. As you progress in your career, your philosophy can and should evolve to match your new values. The most important thing is self-awareness. Leaders who are self-aware and have the drive to continuously reflect and evolve are often the most successful. You have to pay attention to your feedback process and make adjustments as needed.

The world needs good leaders in every endeavor, so we must continuously strive to become better. Becoming more self-aware, having a sound leadership philosophy, and committing to a process that gives you accurate feedback are the keys to success.

Questions to Ponder

"Strive not to be a success but rather to be of value."
—Albert Einstein

What is your leadership philosophy? Does this represent the best you can do? Can you live by this philosophy? Is your leadership philosophy something that is valued or needed in your organization?

SECTION 6
CONCLUSION

"We need great questions in order to know what to do with all the information at our fingertips."
—Warren Berger

CHAPTER 20
THE YEAR AHEAD—
WHAT DO YOU NEED TO PROSPER?

The beginning of a new year is a convenient time to pause, reflect, and determine how to become a more successful you. But your "new year" can start anytime. The key here is to become more self-aware, so you can develop a straightforward and honest understanding of what makes you tick.

January 1 is a good time to reflect on any issues that have held you back and weakened your results in the past year; however, there is nothing magical about January 1, so this is an exercise you can start at any moment. Here's a quick way to reflect, learn, and grow. Ask yourself the following questions about the previous year:

1. What went right?
2. What went wrong? Why?
3. Where am I in my career and personal development?
4. How can I get better tomorrow?

Put the answer to the last question on a card you can carry with you, or post it in a place where you can see it every day. Then, act on it. This is a simple, yet powerful solution busy people can use to quickly determine what they need to prosper.

You cannot really create fundamental change in your life and stop any insecurities from imprisoning you until you change the way you think about your life.

SOMETHING TO MAKE YOU ACT NOW

I hope these chapters have provided valuable advice you can put into practice immediately. Transforming yourself and the members of your organization into proactive, positive agents of change doesn't happen overnight; it's a continuous process of self-improvement. I'm confident that with the right mindset, you can achieve your goals and become less stressed, more focused, and happier in your personal and professional life.

As an extra incentive to begin your journey toward self-awareness, I am offering all first-time book readers a complimentary registration to any of my webinars. Or we can talk about your goals, what's holding you back, and how you can take control of *your* journey. Contact me at soniagartside.com/contact to schedule your thirty-minute consultation.

Thank you for reading
Workplace Anxiety: How to Refuel and Re-engage
If you enjoyed this book, please leave an online review.

KEEP IN TOUCH WITH SONIA LAYNE-GARTSIDE
Website: www.soniagartside.com
Instagram: @soniagartside and @workplaceanxiety
Twitter: @soniagartside

ENDNOTES

Chapter 1: The Mindset That Will (Quickly) Improve Your Work

1. Jim Harter, "Employee Engagement on the Rise in the U.S.," Gallup, 2018, https://news.gallup.com/poll/241649/employee-engagement-rise.aspx
2. Jacob Morgan, "Why the Millions We Spend on Employee Engagement Buy Us So Little," Harvard Business Review, March 10th, 2017, https://hbr.org/2017/03/why-the-millions-we-spend-on-employee-engagement-buy-us-so-little
3. Jim Harter, "4 Factors Driving Record-High Employee Engagement in U.S.," Gallup, 2020, https://www.gallup.com/workplace/284180/factors-driving-record-high-employee-engagement.aspx
4. Dalecarnegie.com, "Recognizing Leadership Blind Spots And Discovering the Road to Motivating Your Employees Whitepaper," dalecarnegie.com, 2017, https://www.dalecarnegie.com/en/resources/recognizing-leadership-blind-spots?utm_source=solaweb&utm_medium=download-page&utm_campaign=r_whitepapers&utm_content=f_911075

5   Tinypulse.com, "The 2019 Employee Engagement Report: The End of Employee Loyalty," tinypulse.com, 2019, https://www.tinypulse.com/hubfs/EE%20Report%202019.pdf

Chapter 2: Three Awesome Tips to Make You Comfortable with Uncertainty

6   A neuroscientist gives a short primer on the brain's emotional processor, "The Amygdala in 5 Minutes," https://bigthink.com/videos/the-amygdala-in-5-minutes
7   Hara Estroff Marano, "Our Brain's Negative Bias," Psychology Today, published June 20, 2003 - last reviewed on June 9, 2016, https://www.psychologytoday.com/us/articles/200306/our-brains-negative-bias
8   Lou Adler, "New Survey Reveals 85% of All Jobs are Filled Via Networking," LinkedIn.com, February 29, 2016, https://www.linkedin.com/pulse/new-survey-reveals-85-all-jobs-filled-via-networking-lou-adler/
9   Dweck, Carol S. 2007, "Mindset: The New Psychology of Success," Ballantine Books; https://www.amazon.com/Mindset-Psychology-Carol-S-Dweck-ebook/dp/B000FCKPHG

Chapter 6: Expert Advice—Do You Know What Great Negotiators Do?

10   Karass, Chester L., 1996, "In Business As in Life, You Don't Get What You Deserve, You Get What You Negotiate," Stanford Street Press

11 Editors: Edwin A. Locke, Gary P. Latham, 2012, "New Developments in Goal Setting and Task Performance", Publisher: Routledge, pp.397-414

Chapter 8: How to Really Listen Better to Everyone

12 Leon Watson, "Humans have shorter attention span than goldfish, thanks to smartphones," The Telegraph newspaper, May 2015, https://www.telegraph.co.uk/science/2016/03/12/humans-have-shorter-attention-span-than-goldfish-thanks-to-smart/

Chapter 9: How to Channel Anger in a Healthy and Powerful Way

13 Rui Fan, Jichang Zhao Yan Chen, Ke Xu, "Anger is More Influential Than Joy: Sentiment Correlation in Weibo," PLoS ONE 9(10): e110184, 2014. https://arxiv.org/abs/1309.2402

Chapter 10: Bottom Line—How to Thrive in a Bureaucracy

14 Maria Konnikova, "How People Learn to Become Resilient," newyorker.com, February 11, 2015, https://www.newyorker.com/science/maria-konnikova/the-secret-formula-for-resilience

Chapter 12: Actually, This Is Why You're Not at Peak Productivity

15 World Cancer Research Fund/American Institute for Cancer Research, "Diet, Nutrition, Physical Activity and

Cancer: A Global Perspective," Washington DC: AICR, 2007, https://www.wcrf.org/dietandcancer

16 Marina Watson Peláez, "Plan Your Way to Less Stress, More Happiness," time.com, May 31, 2011, https://healthland.time.com/2011/05/31/study-25-of-happiness-depends-on-stress-management/

17 Fastcompany.com, "Secrets Of The Most Productive People," November 18, 2014, https://www.fastcompany.com/3038214/secrets-of-the-most-productive-people?utm_source=mailchimp&utm_medium=email&utm_campaign=colead-weekly-newsletter&position=2&partner=newsletter&campaign_date=11242014the

Chapter 13: How to Deal with the Messy Middle—Practical Advice

18 Amy Summerville, "Is Comparison Really the Thief of Joy?," March 21, 2019, https://www.psychologytoday.com/us/blog/multiple-choice/201903/is-comparison-really-the-thief-joy

Chapter 14: How to Lead in an Uncertain World

19 Matt Weinberger, "CEO Satya Nadella succinctly explained the secret of Microsoft's turnaround: 'No status quo'," January 26, 2017, https://www.businessinsider.com/microsoft-ceo-satya-nadella-on-how-he-approaches-growth-2017-1

20 Eugene Kim, "Microsoft has a strange new mission statement," June 25, 2015, https://www.businessinsider.com/microsoft-ceo-satya-nadella-new-company-mission-internal-email-2015-6

Chapter 15: How to Harness Organizational Chaos during Transitions

21 Susan Fowler, "Reflecting On One Very, Very Strange Year At Uber," February 19, 2017, https://www.susanjfowler.com/blog/2017/2/19/reflecting-on-one-very-strange-year-at-uber

22 Dylan Walsh, "Why Uncertainty Makes Us Less Likely to Take Risks," June 1, 2017, https://www.gsb.stanford.edu/insights/why-uncertainty-makes-us-less-likely-take-risks

Chapter 16: How to Give Feedback That Gets Results without Conflict

23 Andrew Martins, "Good Employee Experience Boosts Engagement," August 22, 2019, https://www.businessnewsdaily.com/15272-employee-experience-engagement.html

24 Kendra Cherry, "What Is the Negativity Bias?," April 11, 2019, https://www.verywellmind.com/negative-bias-4589618

Chapter 17: This Will Make You a Clear Communicator

25 Christine Comaford, "SmartTribes: How Teams Become Brilliant Together," (Portfolio, 2013), https://www.amazon.com/SmartTribes-Teams-Become-Brilliant-Together/dp/159184648X

Chapter 18: This Is Why Great Leaders Focus on Customer Service

26 Toma Kulbyte, "37 Customer Experience Statistics You Need to Know for 2020," January 22, 2020, https://www.superoffice.com/blog/customer-experience-statistics/

27 Fred Reicheld, "Presription for Cutting Costs: Loyal Relationships," Bain & Company Inc, Harvard Business School Publishing, September 2001, http://www2.bain.com/Images/BB_Prescription_cutting_costs.pdf

28 Murphy & Murphy, "Leading on the Edge of Chaos," Prentice Hall Press; 1st edition (June 15, 2002), https://www.amazon.com/Leading-Edge-Chaos-Critical-Elements/dp/0735203121

29 Karl Albrecht, "The Only Thing That Matters: Bringing the Power of the Customer into the Center of Your Business," Harpercollins; 1st edition (May 1, 1992), https://www.amazon.com/Only-Thing-That-Matters-Bringing/dp/0887305415/ref=sr_1_1?keywords=Albrecht+Customer&qid=1581460096&s=books&sr=1-1

www.ingramcontent.com/pod-product-compliance
Lightning Source LLC
Chambersburg PA
CBHW021410290426
44108CB00010B/462